Louis Weber, CEO
Publications International, Ltd.
7373 North Cicero Avenue
Lincolnwood, Illinois 60712

www.pilbooks.com

Manufactured in China.

8 7 6 5 4 3 2 1

ISBN-13: 978-1-4508-0574-2
ISBN-10: 1-4508-0574-4

WAYS YOUR DOG MAKES YOU SMILE

Written by
Holli Fort
Trisha L. M. Frederick
Paul Seaburn

new seasons®

Don't worry, I'll tell you when the **scary** part is over and you can **open** your eyes again.

I may not be able to get away from it **all**, but this at least gets me away from the **cat**.

How many dogs does it take to change a roll of **toilet paper**? Yeah, I've heard that one before.

Blossom watched as
the grass turned **green**
again and knew she had
much **work** to do.

In the **battle** between Sparky and the handheld showerhead, Sparky **lost**.

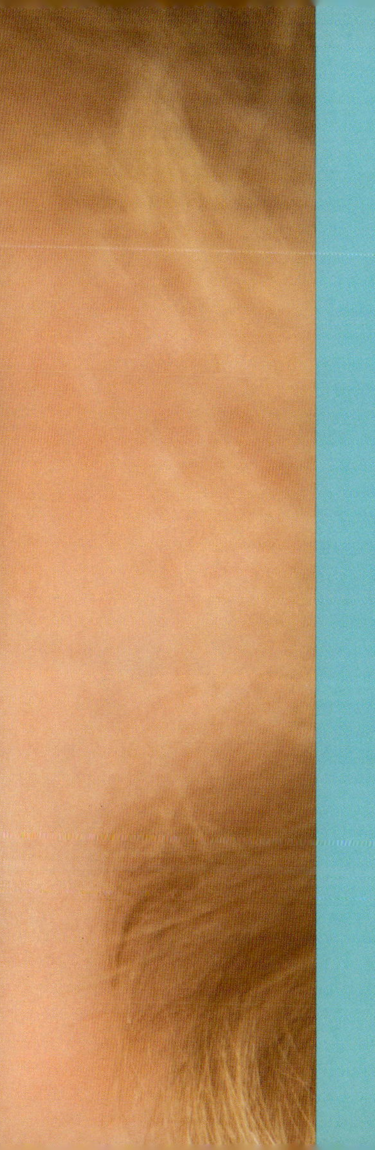

I'm not sure what it is. It smells like **milk**, but it doesn't look like a cat.

What?
I have something on my **face**?

Bruiser was
the canine **taxi**
service's **best**
customer.

It may look like he needs
his **pulse** checked, but really
it's a **blissful** stillness.

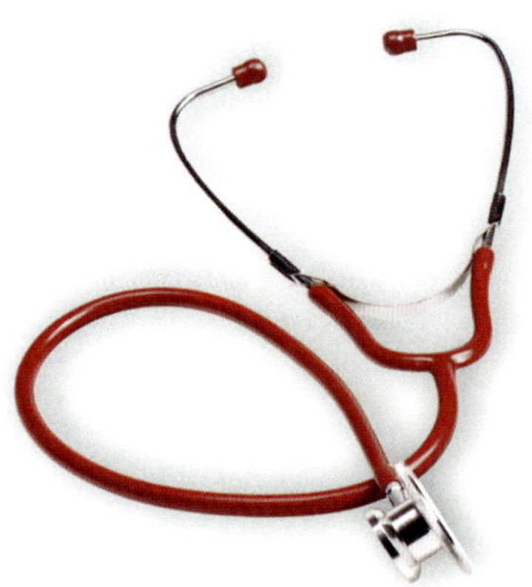

Buster lived in a house
with **newborn triplets**,
and the **sleepless nights**
were really starting
to wear on him.

So many **choices**,
so little **time** . . .

The **Witness Protection Program** isn't all it's cracked up to be.

Maybe **this** will make up for what I did to her **garden**.

There they go **again**! How many times do you think they'll walk by, calling our names, before they **notice** us?

I don't think this girl **behind** me fully understands the rules of **tug-of-war**.

Who is that handsome devil
in the mirror? **Rawr.**

If you're going to cut
my fur this **short**, I'm going
to need some **pants**!

Oh, we ain't got a **barrel** of money,
Maybe we're furry and funny
But we're doing a trick
Fetchin' a stick
Side by side.

Fluff never actually drank
from it, but he loved to see
the **look** on his owner's face
when he **licked his lips.**

Sister? I thought she was a **chew toy**!

My **groomer** says it's the latest style.
She calls it a **Mohound.**

There aren't any **drugs** in this one, but I think we should confiscate this suspicious-looking imported **salami.**

Is this someone's idea of a **cruel** joke?

I **hate** going for walks,
but without me, the women
just **ignore** him.

If I lie really still,
I'll **blend** in and they won't
even know I'm here.

Hold this so I can make
a **snow angel-dog**.

You need to **wake up** and eat.
Have you seen the size
of the **fat cat** next door?

I guess I was **sick** the day they covered this in **obedience school.**

Mid-sneeze, Copper was distracted by a **butterfly** landing on his nose.

offee

I'm meaner than a **junkyard dog** before I have my first cup of coffee in the morning.

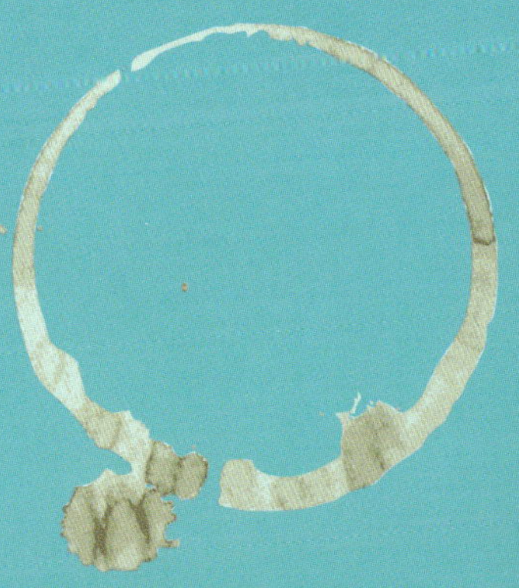

I'll **move** as soon as you do something about that **spider** in my bed.

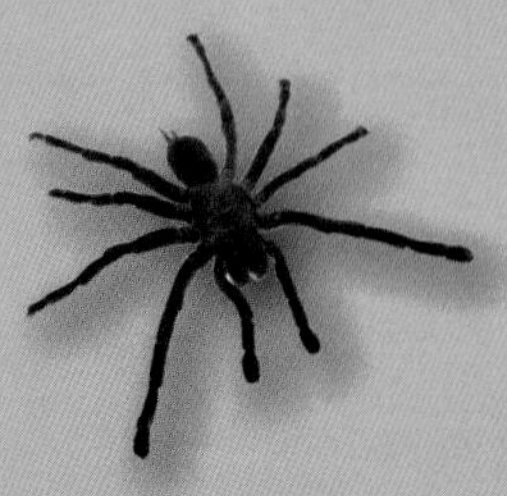

I don't **believe** you used to race. You don't look anything like a **greyhound**.

Get back on **your side.** You're over the line! **Mommm!**

What? You were expecting
me to carry it with my **tail**?

Beats me. Either somebody threw a **ball** or they heard an electric **can opener**.

Why should I bring it back to you? You're just going to **throw** it again.

PHOTO CREDITS:

FRONT COVER: **DigitalVision**

BACK COVER: **Thinkstock**

Alaska Photography; Brand X Pictures; CutCaster; DigitalVision; Fotolia; Getty Images: Charles Briscoe-Knight; Julie Christe; Fry Design Ltd.; Annie Katz; Patti McConville; Gen Nishino; Michelle Pedone; Stephanie Rausser; **Media Bakery; Photodisc; PhotoSpin; Shutterstock; Thinkstock**